P9-CQB-335

IMAGINE THAT!

Activities and Adventures in SURREALISM

JOYCE RAIMONDO

Watson-Guptill Publications/New York

This book is dedicated
to my parents,
Mario and Elizabeth
Raimondo,
who encouraged me
to be the artist I am.

Copyright © 2004 by Joyce Raimondo

First published in 2004 by Watson-Guptill Publications
A division of VNU Business Media, Inc.
770 Broadway, New York, N.Y. 10003
www.watsonguptill.com

All rights reserved. No part of this publication may be reproduced or used in any form or by any means—graphic, electronic, or mechanical, including photocopying, recording, taping, or information storage and retrieval systems—without written permission from the publisher.

Step-by-step artwork by Joyce Raimondo. Photographs of three-dimensional children's art by Rachel Motivitz (pages 30–33, 36–39) and Walter Weissman (pages 31 lower right, 33 lower right, and 37, top three images).

Photo credits: Cover and page 9, *The Persistence of Memory* by Salvador Dalí. Digital image © The Museum of Modern Art/Licensed by SCALA/Art Resource, NY; © 2003 Salvador Dalí, Gala-Salvador Dalí Foundation/Artists Rights Society (ARS), New York. Page 15: *Personal Values* by René Magritte. © 2003 Artists Rights Society (ARS), New York. Page 21: *The Couple* by Max Ernst. Museum Boijmans Van Beuningen, Rotterdam. Page 27: *Carnival of Harlequin* by Joan Miró. Albright-Knox Art Gallery, Buffalo, NY, Room of Contemporary Art Fund, 1940. © 2003 Successío Miró/Artists Rights Society (ARS), New York/ADAGP, Paris. Page 35: *Object* by Meret Oppenheim. © 2003 Artists Rights Society (ARS), New York/ProLitteris, Zürich. Page 41: *Self-Portrait on the Borderline Between Mexico and the United States* by Frida Kahlo. © 2003 Banco de México Diego Rivera & Frida Kahlo Museums Trust. Av. Cinco de Mayo No. 2, Col. Centro, Del. Cuauhtémoc, México, D.F. Photograph: Jacques Rutten.

Every effort has been made to ensure accuracy in this book and to acknowledge all copyright holders. We will be pleased to correct any inadvertent errors or omissions in future editions.

Library of Congress Cataloging-in-Publication Data

Raimondo, Joyce.
  Imagine that! : activities and adventures in surrealism / Joyce
Raimondo.
     p. cm. — (Art explorers)
Summary: An introduction to Surrealism which includes guidance for related activities as well as brief biographies
of six artists: Salvador Dali, Rene Magritte, Max Ernst, Joan Mir, Merit Oppenheim, and Frida Kahlo.
  ISBN 0-8230-2502-0
  1. Surrealism—Juvenile literature. 2. Art appreciation—Juvenile
literature. [1. Surrealism. 2. Art appreciation.] I. Title.
  N6494.S8R35 2004
  709'.04'063—dc22

                                        2003019487

Senior Editor: Julie Mazur
Project Editor: Laaren Brown
Designer: Edward Miller
Production Manager: Ellen Greene
The typefaces in this book include Futura, Typography of Coop, and Ad Lib.

Manufactured in Singapore

First printing, 2004

1 2 3 4 5 6 7 / 10 09 08 07 06 05 04

Contents

Note to Adults: Help Your Child Explore Surrealism 4
Note to Kids: Welcome to the World of Imagination 6

Picturing Dreams—Salvador Dalí 8
    Seeing Double 10
    Dream Journey 12

Everyday Mysteries—René Magritte 14
    Dream House 16
    Look Up! 18

Spark Your Imagination—Max Ernst 20
    Amazing Art Game 22
    Second Look 24

Creatures Featured—Joan Miró 26
    Creature Craze 28
    Collograph Creatures 30
    Fantastic Figures 32

You're Seeing Things—Meret Oppenheim 34
    Food Fantasy 36
    Mystery Box 38

Who Am I?—Frida Kahlo 40
    Drawing Memories 42
    Me and My World 44

Artist Biographies 46

About the Author 48
Acknowledgments 48

Help Your Child Explore Surrealism

Imagine That! invites children to enter the fantastic world of Surrealism and use it as a **springboard for their own creativity**. The discussions in this book encourage children to **examine** works of art and **develop their own personal interpretations**. Related projects, inspired by Surrealist ideas, guide children in an exploration of their **imagination and dreams**.

Surrealism comes full circle

Many Surrealists celebrated the playfulness of children's art and looked to it for its **spontaneous and imaginative** approach. *Imagine That!* comes full circle, asking children to do what comes naturally: delve into the realms of imagination and play through art. Some of the projects ask children to **try actual working methods** designed by the Surrealists to inspire creativity, such as collage, automatic drawing, and art games. Others invite children to **explore concepts developed by Surrealists,** such as thinking about the world in terms of opposites, creating unusual juxtapositions, recording memory and fantasy, and exploring dream imagery.

What do you see in this picture?

The Surrealists believed that the way we see things depends on our individual perceptions. They wanted their artworks to puzzle us and jar our imagination. The questions in this book motivate creative thinking by asking children to talk or write about what they see in art. Let go of your own preconceived ideas about what the artwork means to you, and listen to the children's insights. **Affirm their interpretations**, and ask them to go further with their ideas. When working in a group, **encourage different opinions** about what the picture might mean. Older children may want to research the artists' lives, and they can start with the biographical information in the back of this book.

Everyone is creative

The art instructions in this book guide young artists on **a journey** of discovery. When starting an art project, begin with a lively conversation to **spark ideas**. Ask children what happens in their dreams or discuss an artwork related to the project. Then demonstrate specific techniques while emphasizing play and experimentation. For example, encourage children to rearrange magazine pictures in different ways before gluing them down, or rework their clay spontaneously before defining a sculpture. **Everyone has his or her own way of making things**, and telling children how they should make art stifles creativity. Celebrate the expressive ideas of the child—creativity is a gift to be nurtured in everyone.

Surrealism and the Art of Imagination

Surrealism was an artistic and literary movement that emerged in reaction to the devastation of World War I. Artists responded to the horrors of war by challenging the prevalent norms of society and its values. With a spirit of idealism, artists and writers shared a belief that they could change the world by freeing the unconscious mind from rational thought. In 1924, the French poet André Breton founded the first official Surrealist group in Paris. It was comprised of gifted writers and poets; later, visual artists joined the movement.

Within the movement of Surrealism, there was a rich diversity in approach and style. For some artists, the Surrealist attack on prevalent values involved an element of surprise in which they sought to release their creativity from rational control. They practiced automatic techniques—writing, speaking, or making art without thinking about what they were creating, allowing images and ideas to flow freely from their imagination. Often they then worked back into a painting with deliberation to "pull out" fantastic imagery.

Influenced by Sigmund Freud's notion that the subconscious mind is expressed in dreams, Surrealists drew upon the realm of the inner mind and dreams. Some painted bizarre scenes with minute detail and heightened realism that added to the paintings' shock value. They sought to jar our perception of everyday things by creating unusual juxtapositions of images or actual objects, changing their appearance, scale, or placement. By opening a door to the realm of imagination, the Surrealists had an international impact on the arts, and their work still has an important influence on art today. *Imagine That!* highlights major artists who represent key Surrealist ideas: Salvador Dalí, René Magritte, Max Ernst, and Meret Oppenheim. Also included are Joan Miró and Frida Kahlo, who were not official members but made significant contributions to the movement.

Welcome to the World

What can happen in your **imagination** that is impossible in real life? Maybe you ride on a **magic** carpet or walk a dog on the moon. It's fun to **daydream**. Look up at the clouds. Can you see all kinds of animals in the sky?

Do you **dream** at night when you sleep? What unusual things happen in your dreams? Perhaps you fly across the sky or sit on a rainbow. Have you ever had a **nightmare**? What was it like? Maybe you imagined that a monster was chasing you, and you woke up in a fright.

You're about to enter a world of imagination and dreams created by **Surrealist artists**. In their artworks, you might visit a place where everything melts or one where strange creatures fly.

The Surrealists invented all kinds of new ways of making art to **spark creativity**. Some Surrealists made **automatic pictures**. They painted or drew without looking at what they were making or stopping to think about how it would turn out. Some wrote **nonsense stories** by letting any words that popped into their heads flow out, no matter how silly they seemed. One artist even swung paint from a can and let it drip all over just to see where it would land.

Some Surrealists painted their **weird** dreams and nightmares. Even though the world they

# of Imagination

painted was completely **make-believe**, they painted their dreams with such detail that they looked real. They shook up the way we see ordinary things by **mixing everything up**! Picture a cup that is larger than your bed or a gigantic comb that you can climb onto. Or how about a cat's head on a human body—with wings! The Surrealists wanted their artworks to open our imagination and help us **see the world in a new way**.

This book invites you to do just that—**dive into your imagination**. Make up stories about the artworks in this book. Then create your own way-out art inspired by the Surrealists. Scribble a doodle, splash some paint, cut up a magazine, and surprise yourself. Create art that is so **silly** it makes you laugh out loud. Or paint a **scary** picture that sends chills down your spine. Your art can be as **strange** or **different** as you want it to be. Anything can happen in your art—so **let your imagination run free**!

PICTURING DREAMS

SALVADOR DALÍ

Salvador Dalí painted what he saw in his dreams and his inner mind. In this picture, we see the rocky cliffs of the Catalonian seashore in Spain, where Dalí grew up. Yet everything seems strange. Clocks seem to be melting. A mysterious object sits in the center of the painting. Some people think it is Dalí's face in profile. Do you see its long eyelashes and funny-looking tongue? Others think it is a strange animal. Dalí wanted his pictures to puzzle us. He left it up to us to decide what his pictures mean. As you can see, he painted his imaginary scenes with great detail. The soft objects and shadows look so real, it is as if we could step right into this dream world and touch them.

Close your eyes and picture yourself traveling to a make-believe place. Open your eyes and imagine that this is where you landed.

- Look all around. What do you **see** here?
- What would it be like to be in this **place**?
- Notice the **clocks**. What is **unusual** about them?
- Why are the clocks soft? How would you explain this **mystery**?
- Take a close look at the **large object** on the ground. What could it be?
- Find a **tree**. What is **strange** about it?
- Travel to the **background** of the picture. What do you see there?
- What is the **weather** like in this place?
- What **time** of day or night is it? How can you tell?

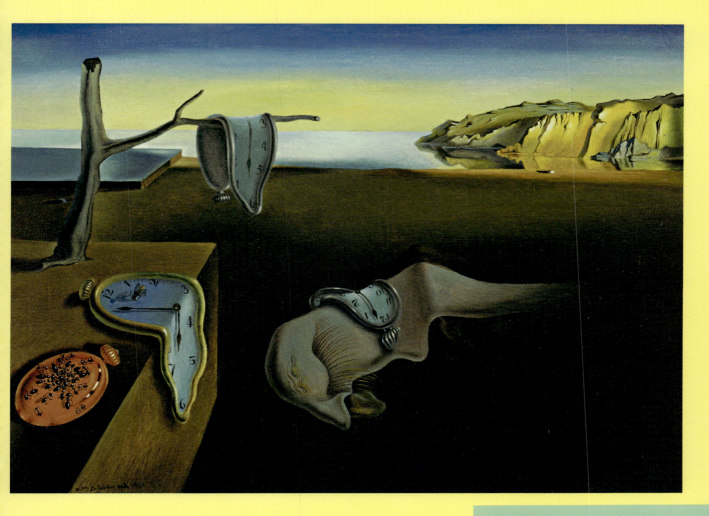

The Persistence of Memory, 1931
oil on canvas, 9 ½ x 13 inches
The Museum of Modern Art, New York

- What other odd things do you see in the picture?
- What about this place is like a **dream**?
- Would you want to **be in this picture**? Why or why not?

Make up a story about your **adventures** in this strange land.

**Travel to the land
of your dreams.**
The art projects in this section invite
you to visit places in your imagination.

Seeing Double

Make a collage of a dream place filled with double images.
Take a close look at Dalí's dream painting on page 9. Many things can be seen in different ways. At first the clocks might appear to be melting. Or maybe they are made of soft rubber or floppy pancakes! Some people see the strange object in the middle of the picture as a horse with a clock for a saddle. Others see it as a duck, or a platypus, a blanket, or a funny face. Even the cliffs in the background might look like animal shapes. Stretch your imagination as you make your own dream place filled with double pictures.

1. Make the place. Paste paper or a magazine image across the bottom of your picture for the ground.

2. Trick the eye. Cut out magazine pictures of things that can stand in for something else. For example, wheels might be made of round clocks, a car might be made out of a cell phone.

Here are some ideas: Make a sun out of something really strange. Show a weird flying creature or aircraft. Build a funny car out of unusual things. Create buildings and trees that are out of this world. Imagine treetops made of giant lemons and houses made of American flags. Make a funny person out of pictures that you find.

3. Arrange your pictures to create the imaginary place, then glue them down.

4. Write a story about your picture.

Supplies

Magazines
Scissors
Glue
Paper

Drive in my shoe car!—Timmy, 9

Look out! A hamburger with eyes!—Yanncy, 10

The sun smiles in the dark sky.—Raymond, 11

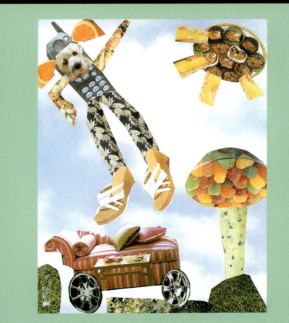

The cell phone dog is flying!—Gabriel, 11

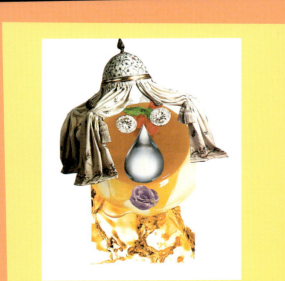

Hair made of curtains!—Joshua, 9

Try this, too!

Strange Faces

Make a face filled with double pictures. Cut a large oval for the head out of a magazine picture. Now find things that can be used for the eyes, nose, mouth, ears, and hair. For example, you might make hair from curtains, eyes from diamonds, and a flower mouth.

Dream Journey

Another Dalí idea

What happens in your dreams that is impossible?

Maybe monsters chase you, or you fly above the trees. Perhaps you visit a land where everything melts or one where cats can fly. Like Dalí, travel into your mind and paint or draw a dream scene.

1. Go on an imaginary trip and draw what you see. Picture yourself flying way above the clouds, far away to a make-believe land. Maybe you travel on a magic carpet or fly with wings. Look out! There is something really funny looking up in the sky. What is it? Now fly down to the ground. Everything looks strange. Picture a place where the shapes of things are mixed up and distorted. Look at my wobbly house with lips for a roof! Any zany thing can happen here. A ballerina has a clock for a head. Make up something funny for your picture and draw what you see on your journey.

2. Paint or color in your picture. It is fun to mix up the colors of things. Look at the purple trees and green clouds!

> What is a television . . . to man, who has only to shut his eyes to see the most inaccessible regions of the seen and the never seen?
> —Salvador Dalí

Supplies

Paper
Drawing materials
Paint
Brushes

Angry ice cream!—Gabriel, 11

Fish swim above crooked buildings.—Mat, 10

Aliens are landing.—Trevor, 10

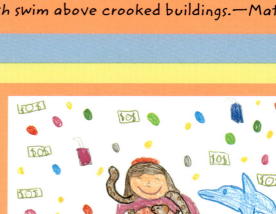

I swam with dolphins. Jumped in the ball pit. Ice-cream shakes melting. Have gold and money. Held python snake in ballerina dress. —Nicole, 9

Try this, too!

Write On!

Like the Surrealists, you can experiment with **automatic writing**. Start writing quickly without stopping to think. Jot down whatever pops into your head no matter how silly it seems—just keep writing. For example, "Boy walked down the street, found a frog, and ate a car." Then make a picture of your crazy writing.

Dream Stories

Write a story about an actual dream or nightmare you've had and paint or draw a picture of it.

EVERYDAY MYSTERIES

RENÉ MAGRITTE

René Magritte created this mysterious scene by changing the size of ordinary things. A giant comb stands on a bed, and a huge glass sits in the center of the room! How can this mystery be explained? Is this a magic room where ordinary things have suddenly become gigantic? Or perhaps it is a dollhouse filled with household objects. Notice the strange walls. Some people think the room is covered in cloud wallpaper. Others imagine it is floating way up in the air.

Magritte looked at the world around him and sketched out his ideas. He made many drawings to plan his mysterious paintings. As you can see, everything in this imaginative room is painted with great detail to look very real.

Imagine if you woke up and your room looked like this! What would you think?

- What **everyday objects** do you see?
- What is the object in the bottom right corner of the picture?
- What are all of these things doing together in the picture?
- **A comb is larger than a bed!** How can it be?
- Notice the **sizes of things**. What is strange about them?
- Can you explain why the sizes of things are so **mixed up**?
- Look into the **cabinet**. What do you notice?
- **Walls are made of clouds!** How can you explain this **mystery**?
- What else is **strange** about this room?

Personal Values, 1952
oil on canvas, 31 1/2 x 39 2/5 inches
San Francisco Museum of Modern Art

- Look closely. How can you tell that the furniture is **inside** a room and not **outside**?
- Use your **imagination**. What would it be like to live in a house like this?
- What would you do with all of these things?

Make up a **story** about this **dream house**.

How can you change your everyday world into a magical place?
Create a mysterious world where everything is the opposite of what you would expect to see and anything is possible.

Dream House

Make art inspired by Magritte

Make a magazine collage of a dream room.

What if you woke up and saw a giant comb on your bed that you could climb on? Imagine that you walked into your house and saw an apple that was so big it touched the ceiling! What if a train zoomed through your living room? Like Magritte, shake up the way ordinary things look. Make a fantasy room where everyday things are seen in crazy mixed-up ways.

1. Make the room. Glue a magazine picture strip along the bottom of your picture to show the floor. Add another picture for the wall. Why not make the room out of something really weird? Picture a floor made of flowers and walls filled with clouds.

2. Clip magazine pictures of things you find indoors, such as furniture. Then cut out things you find outdoors, such as trees, cars, and grass. Also find pictures of everyday objects—sneakers, cups, or food.

3. Turn it inside out! Put things inside the room that belong outside. Maybe a tree grows in your bedroom and a penguin sits on the floor. Change the sizes of things. What if you saw a gigantic tomato on your dresser and a pencil that was large enough to climb on? Put things where they do not belong. What would it be like if furniture hung from the ceiling or a big football was floating above your bed?

4. You can also draw or paint ideas into the picture along with the magazine cut-outs. When you are satisfied with your wacky dream house, glue down the cut-outs.

Supplies

Magazine pictures
Paper
Scissors
Glue
Drawing materials

A giant bird landed in my living room!—Kenneth, 9

Car zooms through the kitchen!—Thomas Z., 8

Crazy flying bathroom.—Thomas D., 8

Right Before My Eyes

Imagine that everything in your house was magically transforming from one thing into another. Make a **metamorphosis** drawing or collage that shows an object that is changing from one thing into something else. For example, Magritte once made a pair of shoes that seemed to be turning into actual feet, and a fish that looked half human.

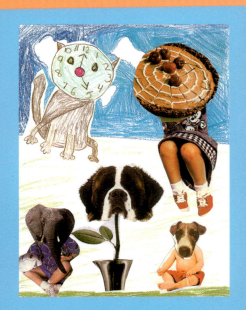

Cat turns into clock and other strange things.—Kyle S., Kyle H., Kimberly, and Keith, 8—10

Look Up!

Another Magrite idea

Make a cut-paper collage of an out-of-this-world sky.

Picture your bedroom floating in the air, or walls made out of clouds. Travel out the window to a castle way up high. We know these things are impossible, yet in Magritte's paintings they look very real. Magritte loved to make pictures where everything is the opposite of what you would expect. In his paintings, he made wondrous skies filled with mysterious things. Why not create your own sky, where everything is mixed up and anything can float or fly?

1. Brainstorm. What do you normally see in the sky? What do you usually see on the ground?

2. Cut paper shapes for your picture of clouds, the sun, houses, or other things you want to use.

3. Arrange the pictures to create a fantasy sky. Here are some ideas: What if everything that is normally on the ground was suddenly in the sky? Picture trees growing in the air and flowers rising out of clouds. Put things on the ground that belong in the sky. What would it be like if the sun shone from the street and stars walked next to you? What if houses could float and dogs flew way up high? Make it rain something really weird. Yummm—it is raining ice-cream cones! Why not make it rain up instead of down?

4. Glue everything down to make your collage.

 ▶  ▶

Supplies

Colored paper
Scissors
Glue

To be a Surrealist... means barring from your mind all remembrance of what you have seen, and being always on the lookout for what has never been.—René Magritte

A flower grows from grass in the sky.—Daniela, 11

Is this outer space or under water?—Jana, 11

Is it raining up or down?—Austin, 11

Sun and moon shine on the night surfer.—Christopher D., 10

Try this, too!

Night and Day

In his famous picture *Empire of Light*, Magritte painted a bright daytime sky—yet everything below it on the street was as dark as night. Imagine a world where night and day happen at the same time. What would it be like if the sun shone in a night sky while the moon and stars were out? What if you surfed at the beach in the dark and wore sunglasses at night? Make a cut-paper collage picture where nighttime and daytime are completely mixed up.

SPARK YOUR IMAGINATION

MAX ERNST

For Max Ernst, art was an adventure. He wanted his pictures to flow freely from his mind without controlling exactly what they would be. He invented all kinds of new ways to make art to inspire his wild imagination. Sometimes he swung paint from a can and let it spill all over, or he might press materials onto a wet painting to get surprising effects. He also made hundreds of collages by cutting and pasting magazine pictures in strange combinations to tell bizarre stories. In his art, we find imaginary beings, monsters, and fantastic dream scenes.

Look closely at this painting. You will notice many things that are strange. Who might these odd people be? One has a blue body and a long head. The other seems to have a lace face and no hair! The pair seems to be made of scraps of lace that have been cut and pasted together, like a collage. But Ernst actually painted this funny-looking couple.

Enter the world of imagination and meet some strange beings.

- Take a close look at these **unusual people**. Notice the figure on the left. What is **funny** about this **person**? Look at the **face**. How would you describe it?
- Look at the other person. What is **strange** about the **body**? How would you describe the **head**? What is this person **doing**?
- Do you think these people are **men or women**? What gives you that idea?
- **Who** are these people? Why do you think they look this way?
- What do you think they are **doing together** in the picture?

The Couple, 1925
oil on canvas, 40 x 56 inches
Museum Boijmans Van Beuningen, Rotterdam,
The Netherlands

- Look into the **background** of the picture.
  Notice some of the details. What do you see there?
- Where is this scene taking **place**? What seems to be
  make-believe about this place?
- **What will happen** next?

Make up a **story** about these **strange
people** in this strange place.

**Dive into the world of
your own imagination.**
Try surprising ways of making art
that free your creative mind.

Amazing Art Game

Play this famous art game. With a group of friends, create a surprise creature!

Ernst loved to create all kinds of imaginary beings invented from his head. Sometimes he played art games with his friends to surprise himself with new ideas. In this game, one person draws the head, another person draws the body, and a third person draws the legs. At the end, all the parts are shown to reveal a surprise creature. While you are playing, do not look at what other people have drawn—wait until the paper is unfolded!

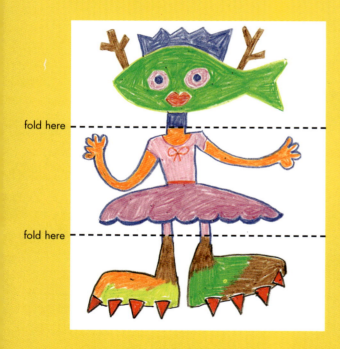

fold here

fold here

1. Play with three or more people. Each person gets a sheet of paper. Fold your sheet into three equal parts. Then unfold the paper and lay it flat.

2. Draw a weird head in the top section. Maybe it has green skin and antlers or spiky blue hair. Draw a neck with two small lines onto the middle section. This will show the next person where he or she should continue the body.

3. Now, fold back the top of the paper. Give your folded sheet to the person sitting next to you.

4. Add a wacky body in the middle section of the paper you just got. Draw the tummy of a ballerina, a cow, a clown, or anything else. When you are finished, draw little lines onto the bottom section so the next person will know where to connect the legs. Fold up the paper and pass it on again.

5. Draw wild legs and feet in the bottom section. You might draw dinosaur claws, horse hooves, or a pair of bell-bottom jeans!

6. Surprise! When everyone is finished, open up the papers. What weird, wacky, wild figures have you created?

Supplies

Paper
Colored pencils,
  crayons,
  or markers

It's a groovy rooster!—Chris, Daria, and Ashley, 11–12

Funny clockface dude. —Sean, Daria, and Lucas, 11–12

Elephant ears wear a lot of earrings.—Mata, Nhailinger, and Chris, 11–12

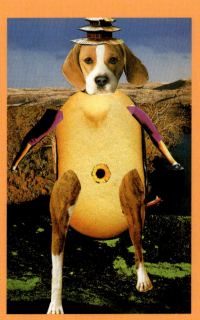

Cookie dog with flower belly button.—Antonio, 9

Try this, too!

All Mixed Up

Like Ernst, create a make-believe figure. Clip magazine pictures you can use for the head, body, arms, and legs. For example, you can make a body out of a giant cookie, add a dog's head, and use a house for a hat! You can also make a mixed-up person-animal. Start with an image of a person and then make it really weird by changing one thing. Imagine a policeman with a cat's head or a baby with wings.

Though it is the feathers that make the plumage, it is not the paste that makes the collage.—Max Ernst

23

Second Look

Explore the art of frottage! Make crayon rubbings of objects, then "pull out" fantastic pictures.

One day Max Ernst looked down at the wooden floor. He noticed patterns in the wood grain. He placed a sheet of paper on the floorboards and rubbed over them with a soft drawing material. He called this new way of making art **frottage**— French for "rubbing." Sometimes he looked into the rubbings and added marks to create imaginary beings or places.

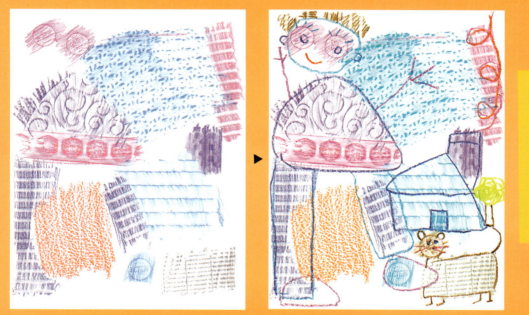

Supplies

Textured objects
Paper
Crayons
Scissors
Glue

1. Collect textured objects. Find things around your home that have bumpy or raised surfaces. Like Ernst, you can use wood, string, seashells, leaves, and bark. You can also try coins, lace, netting, doilies, or corrugated cardboard.

2. Rub it out! Firmly hold paper over one of the objects. Rub back and forth with the side of a crayon. Watch the texture of the object emerge. Experiment with other items on the same paper.

3. Take a second look! Look into all of the patterns and textures. Can you find a picture of a face or an animal? What else might you see?

4. Draw back into the picture. Create imaginary creatures, plants, flowers, houses, or anything you see. You can also cut up your rubbings and glue them together in new ways.

We found animals in the picture.
—Raquel and Timmy, 7 and 9

I made a rainbow house and a car.
—Timmy, 9

I used my rubbings to make a cute dog. —Raquel, 7

Try this, too!

Paint Surprises

To spark his imagination, Ernst sometimes placed a sheet of paper on a wet painting and pulled the paper away. Then he worked back into the painting to create imaginary creatures and places. This kind of pressed painting is called **decalcomania**. Try it for yourself! Freely brush or pour paint onto paper. Then press a second piece of paper over your wet painting. Lift up the paper. What do you see? Can you find silly faces, strange creatures, plants, or flowers? Paint or draw back into your picture to "pull" out images.

Paint squiggles turn into wiggly creatures. —Michael, 9

CREATURES FEATURED

JOAN MIRÓ

The Spanish artist Joan Miró painted a world of wondrous creatures that seem to dance before our eyes. He got ideas for his pictures by remembering his family's farm, drawing inspiration from the animals, plants, and insects he saw there. Rather than paint nature exactly as it looks, Miró invented all kinds of colorful creatures. As you can see, Miró especially liked to paint flowing curvy shapes. They seem to wiggle and squiggle in a carnival of imagination.

Even though Miró painted in a playful style, if you look closely, you will notice that he carefully arranged the shapes in this picture. Notice all the circles that seem to move across the painting and the curvy shape in the center that forms a cross.

Welcome to a world of imaginary creatures.

- Play a **looking game**. Describe one of the creatures in the painting in **detail**. Ask a friend to guess which creature you are talking about. If he or she cannot find it right away, add more **clues**.
- Can you **find a creature** that seems to be made from **a guitar** and has a **circle** for a head? Here's a clue: Its face is **half red** and **half blue**.
- Find a creature that is coming **out of a box**. It has two **colored wings**, one yellow and one blue. It has black **antennae** and two **tiny black arms**.
- Look for two creatures in the front of the picture. They have **striped bodies** and **curvy arms**. What do you think they are doing?
- Notice the **ladder**. What do you see as you **climb to the top** of it?

Carnival of Harlequin, 1924–1925
oil on canvas, 26 x 35 5/8 inches
Albright-Knox Art Gallery, Buffalo, New York

- What are all these crazy-looking creatures **doing**?
- What **musical instruments** can you find? Why do you think they are in the picture?
- Make up a **title** for this scene. Why would you call it that?

Write a **story** about these creatures. Tell about where they are from and **what is happening** in the picture.

Create your own imaginary creatures.
Paint, print, and sculpt all kinds of fantastic beings.

Creature Craze

Make a watercolor resist painting of a wondrous world filled with imaginary creatures.

Picture a guitar that dances or a snake that flies. Create a picture filled with wild creatures invented from your head. You can begin by drawing shapes for your imaginary creatures, or start with a doodle that you change into a creature.

1. Make a line drawing with crayons or oil pastels. Here are some ideas to get started: You can begin by drawing shapes of mixed-up animals. I made a cat with three eyes and a wing! Or make creatures out of musical instruments. A guitar might become a silly face with a long neck. A piano keyboard with legs becomes a funny caterpillar.

2. Let it flow! You can also begin by letting your crayon wander freely around your paper. Do not stop to think about what you are drawing. This free way of drawing without thinking is called **automatic drawing.** Then draw back into the web of lines. "Pull out" images of animals and creatures. Add legs, eyes, feet, or any other parts.

3. When your drawing is finished, lightly paint with watercolor over the lines. Notice how the crayon lines show through and "resist" the watercolor.

Supplies

Crayons or oil pastels
Paper
Watercolor paints
Brushes
Sponges to clean brushes

My father was very realistic...if I said the sky was purple, he made fun of me, which threw me into a rage.—Joan Mir

Colorful animals dance together.—Ashley, 8

Scribbles become a green monster.—Ben, 9

World of one-eyed animals.—Victor, 9

Five eyes and nine legs! What is it?—Rachel, Morrison, Basil, Lauren, and Brooke, 9–12

Try this, too!

Night Visions

Miró painted amazing night skies filled with whimsical creatures and flowing designs. Draw a night sky filled with stars, constellations, planets, and imaginary beings invented from your head. It is fun to draw on black paper with oil pastels or chalk.

Collograph Creatures

Create creatures as you explore the art of collograph printmaking.

In addition to painting, Miró made wild creatures and printed them. (A **print** is made when you make a copy of your artwork.) First Miró glued scrap materials such as wood or wire to a board. Then he rolled ink onto the materials, and pressed a paper against the inky surface. This kind of print is called a **collograph**.

▼

▼

1. Collect textured materials such as rope, netting, corrugated cardboard, bubble wrap, aluminum foil, or wood. Choose materials that will not absorb ink—for example, absorbent fabric or cotton will *not* work.

2. Make your printing plate. Cut your materials into shapes. Arrange them on cardboard to create a strange creature. A piece of corrugated cardboard might be a body, and wood sticks can be legs. You can make a tail with string or rope. Securely tape or glue down the materials.

3. Carefully roll ink onto the materials with a brayer (roller). If you don't have a roller, ask an adult to look in the kitchen for something else you can use. Try not to get the ink on the empty spaces of your cardboard.

4. Place a sheet of paper over the materials. Gently press with your hand or the brayer.

5. Surprise! Lift up the paper to see your print. Repeat the process to print more pictures. Experiment with different kinds of papers, and roll out different colors of ink to get new effects.

Supplies

Water-based printing ink
Brayer (roller)
Textured materials and cardboard shapes
Cardboard for base
Scissors
Glue or tape
Paper

My animal has curly ears and a wagging tail.—Lily, 9

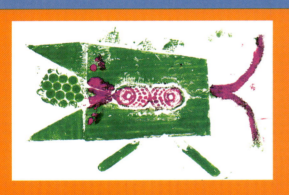

Fish on the move.—Christopher S., 8

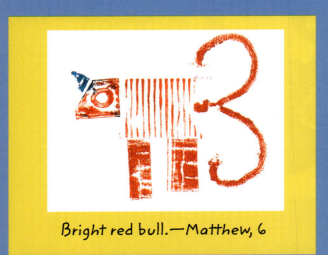

Bright red bull.—Matthew, 6

Try these, too!

Book It!

Like Miró, you can turn your prints into a handmade book. Make a lot of prints or drawings, then arrange them for your pages. Don't forget to make a cover! Punch holes along the edges of the pages and bind them together with string or ribbon. You can add words to tell a story or write a poem.

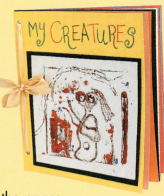

Texture Animals

Miró and the Surrealists loved to use unusual materials to spark new ideas. Look around your house. Collect textured materials such as rough tree bark, soft cotton, smooth fabric, and fuzzy felt. Cut and arrange your materials on cardboard to create a creature. Yarn might be used for a curly tail and buttons for eyes.

Pretty pig with wings.—Brooke, 10

Fantastic Figures

Sculpt a one-of-a-kind make-believe person using clay.

Miró collected stones, branches, and other things and used them to create **imaginary figures**. Then he cast them in bronze. He called his fantasy people "personages." Why not mold your own imaginary person using clay?

1. Form the body. Mold legs, arms, a head, and any other details you like. To add clay pieces, poke a wooden stick or wire through each part. The sticks and wire will support the clay and make the sculpture strong.

2. Make it look really silly or weird. Why not change the shape of things? I made a heart-shaped head and a roly-poly body that wobbles along the ground.

3. Give your figure a funny face. How about fangs and flower eyes? Look closely—a fish and paper clips are popping out of its head.

4. Decorate your figure with all kinds of materials, such as old jewelry, shells, rocks, beads, feathers, pipe cleaners, colored toothpicks, and other stuff.

5. When the clay dries, paint your figure.

Supplies

Self-hardening clay
Clay tools
Wooden sticks or dowels
Pieces of wire
Decorative materials
Paint
Paintbrush

Long ears with
feather earrings!
—Raquel, 7

Say hello to my
square-headed guy.
—Timmy, 9

My good-luck troll.
—Timmy, 9

Try this, too!

Marvelous Monsters

Step into your laboratory and build a fantasy monster
out of materials you find around your home. You
can tape or glue cardboard boxes and tubes
together for the body and head. Then add
smaller parts for the legs and arms. Be
crazy! Decorate it with beads, wrapping paper,
yarn, pipe cleaners, and other fancy materials.
This type of artwork—built from objects—is called
an **assemblage.**

Friendly monster
going to a party.
—Madeline, 7

YOU'RE SEEING THINGS

MERET OPPENHEIM

Imagine drinking from a teacup lined with fur! The Swiss artist Meret Oppenheim made this way-out sculpture by combining everyday items in surprising ways that do not make any sense at all.

Oppenheim got her idea for the sculpture when she was sitting at a café in Paris with the famous artist Pablo Picasso. That day she was wearing a fur-trimmed bracelet. Picasso looked at her bracelet and commented that anything could be covered with fur. Oppenheim replied, "Even this cup and saucer!" Later she bought a teacup and actually lined it with fur. This strange artwork became one of the most famous Surrealist sculptures.

What in the world is going on? Imagine yourself sitting down for a meal and finding this!

- What **objects** do you see here? What seems to be really **weird** about them?
- Picture yourself **drinking** from this cup. Take a sip! What would that be like?
- Would you be able to use a **cup** like this? Why or why not?
- How do you think the artist made this **sculpture**?
- How did she change an **ordinary** object into an **outrageous** work of art?

Object, 1936
fur-lined cup, saucer, and spoon,
overall height 2 7/8 inches
The Museum of Modern Art, New York

- In what ways is this artwork **different** from most sculptures you have seen?
- **Imagine.** What would it be like if everything in the world were made from something **strange and unexpected**? What if buildings were made of chocolate and cars were made of cotton candy?

Invent a **story** about what it would be like to live in a **mixed-up world**.

Go on a search for objects and materials you can use to create your own Surrealist sculptures.
Create outrageous works of art from everyday items that you collect.

Food Fantasy

Combine objects in really weird ways to make a table setting that's out of this world.

Meret Oppenheim and the Surrealists made crazy sculptures by changing the way ordinary things look. Imagine sitting down for a meal made of flowers, or sipping from a cup that's filled with cotton balls. This project invites you to create a crazy, mixed-up, make-believe meal.

▼

▼

1. Find old cups, dishes, bowls, or utensils for your project, or use paper ones. Ask an adult to help you.

2. Gather materials you want to add, such as glitter, cotton, sand, and beads.

3. Use the materials you found to make your dishes really strange. What would it be like if your cup was lined with sandpaper or cotton? What would it be like to eat with a spoon made of feathers and a plate made of rocks?

4. Fill your dishes with fake food made out of wild and wacky materials. For example, imagine dipping your spoon into a cereal bowl filled with glitter or drinking from a glass filled with shiny balls. Make spaghetti out of yarn, pizza out of felt, or mashed potatoes out of cotton balls!

5. Display your table setting on a strange place mat. Choose a surface that's different from what you would expect—such as artificial grass or fake fur!

6. Glue your objects to the place mat. Ask an adult to help you if you need to use hot glue for heavy objects.

Supplies

Dishes and utensils
Found materials
Glue or tape
Scissors

Nobody will give you freedom—you have to take it.
—Meret Oppenheim

Beaded spaghetti and smiling sandwich.

Pompom food and pink ice-cream cone.

Aren't these strange? —Rachel, Gabriel, Carrie, and Gemma's group, 8–12

Alphabet soup and pizza with everything.

A dog's dream. —Timmy, 9

Try this, too!

Weird, Really Weird

Create a Surrealist sculpture by combining objects in unusual ways that do not make sense. What would it be like if dog treats grew on plants? What would it be like to wear a shoe that was filled with rocks? After you decide what objects to combine, glue or tape them together.

Mystery Box

Create a fantasy box filled with unusual treasures.

Meret Oppenheim and other Surrealists loved to collect all kinds of objects and use them to create sculptures. They inspired other artists to do the same. The artist Joseph Cornell collected hundreds of objects that he used to create mysterious boxes. Do you like to collect rocks, shells, charms, and other small stuff? It is fun to collect things and arrange them in a one-of-a-kind treasure box.

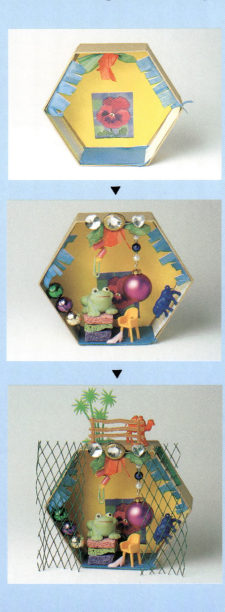

1. **Find a box,** such as a jewelry gift box, a cigar box, a wooden crate, or an ordinary shoebox.

2. **Collect treasures.** Search for old toys, broken jewelry, charms, action figures, game pieces, and other fun stuff. Things you might normally throw away, such as old candy wrappers or used greeting cards, can be recycled for your project.

3. **Prepare the inside of the box.** Paint it or decorate it with fancy collage papers.

4. **Place the objects together in mysterious or silly ways.** For example, I hung a Christmas tree bulb next to a toy frog that's sitting on a stack of sponges.

5. **Attach the objects with glue.** If you need to use hot glue, ask an adult to help.

6. **Decorate or paint the outside.** You can glue other trinkets to the outside of the box. Also, think about how you want to display the box. You can seal it shut and cut a small hole in the cover for a person to peek into. Or cover the box with colored cellophane for extra mystery.

Supplies

Box
Assorted papers
Collection of objects
Glue
Scissors
Paint
Brushes

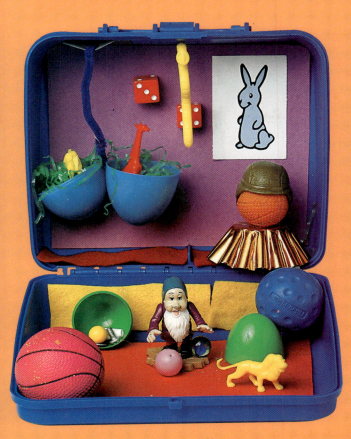

My old toys make a silly scene.—Timmy, 9

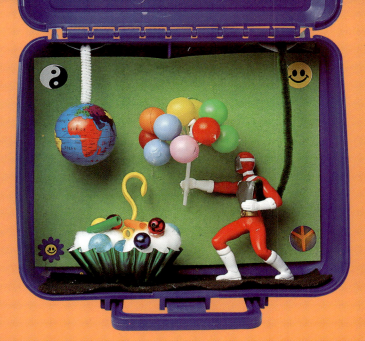

Action figure fights with balloons! —Raquel, 7

Try this, too!

Portrait Box

Make a portrait of someone you know by collecting objects and materials that remind you of that person and then arranging them in a box. A box about a person who loves sports might include balls, trophies, or baseball cards. A box about a baby might include a rattle and a bib. What would you put in a box to make a portrait of yourself?

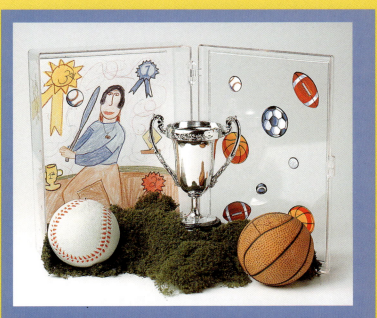

First place! I love sports.—Britney Mae, 11

WHO AM I?

FRIDA KAHLO

Frida Kahlo painted pictures that told about the events of her life. Kahlo painted this picture when she was traveling through the United States with her husband, the artist Diego Rivera, who was working as a muralist. Kahlo longed to return to her homeland, Mexico. Kahlo stands with a Mexican flag in hand, like a statue caught between two worlds. One side of the picture shows her beloved Mexico, with its ancient temples, artifacts, and bright flowers. Travel to the other side and you see a very different place. The American flag floats by smokestacks and skyscrapers in the industrial city of Detroit. Chimneys seem to march like robots and light bulbs grow from the soil instead of plants. Kahlo tells us about her thoughts and feelings in an imaginative way. Notice the sun, spitting fire, and the moon, bowing its head as if it were sad.

This picture is a self-portrait. It tells about the artist who made it, Frida Kahlo. Look at the picture and see if you can figure out the story.

- How would you **describe the place** on the right side? What do you see there? Where is this? How can you tell?
- Travel to the **left side** of the picture. **Where** might this be? What things do you see there?
- What is happening in the **sky**?
- Notice the **objects** along the bottom of the picture. What do you think they are?
- Describe the **woman**. What is she **doing**?
- What is she **wearing**? What do her **clothes** say about her?

Self-Portrait on the Borderline Between Mexico and the United States, 1932
oil on tin, 11 ¾ x 13 ½ inches
Collection of Mr. and Mrs. Manuel Reyero

- What does her **face** tell us about how she feels? What might her **pose** say?
- Look closely. What is she **holding**? What might that mean?
- This picture shows two places that Kahlo lived. Compare the two sides of the picture. How do you think Kahlo **felt** about each place?

Write about **two places** that are important in your life.

Explore the world of your own memories.
Tell stories about your life in imaginative self-portraits.

Drawing Memories

Make art inspired by Kahlo

Paint or draw a picture of a memory.
A **self-portrait** is an artwork that you make about yourself. Like Kahlo, draw or paint a picture about an important memory. What was the happiest day of your life? What was the worst day? Here are some topics: an exciting trip, a fun party, the saddest day ever, something I love to do, my pet and me. Instead of drawing things exactly as they looked, draw how you felt and what you imagined.

1. Think of what you were doing, and show it. For example, when I was a child, I was sick on Halloween. I could not go out to trick-or-treat. So in my picture, I show myself sick in bed.

2. Draw your facial expression. You can show a happy face with a smile, or a sad one with a pout. An angry person might have eyebrows pointing down or a big mouth screaming.

3. Paint the place. Put something in your picture that tells where it is happening. Is it in the city, a park, inside a house, or somewhere else?

4. Draw details to tell the story. Look out the window. Can you figure out what the people are doing? Can you tell what the girl has in her mouth?

5. Imagine! Tell about your thoughts, feelings, or dreams by showing something make-believe. I felt sad and disappointed. So I drew tears pouring out of pumpkins!

Supplies

Paper
Drawing materials or paint

I never painted dreams. I painted my own reality.
—Frida Kahlo

 ▶  ▶

The day I got my horse.—Melissa, 11

Tears for my dog in heaven.—Felicia, 12

I play soccer in the sky!—Erik, 11

My birthday treasure.—Raquel, 7

Treasured Memories

Capture a special day in your life by collecting memory materials. Choose an event such as a birthday party, a special trip, or a sporting event. Collect materials from your special day such as gift wrap, ribbon, and cards, and paste them in a design on a piece of cardboard.

Dream Diary

Frida Kahlo kept wonderful diaries, and so can you. Write stories about what happened during your day and tell about your feelings. Jot down your dreams and fantasies. It is fun to fill a special journal with pictures, scrap materials, photos, and collages.

Me and My World

Make a photo collage about places you love.

Frida Kahlo was proud of her Mexican heritage, and many of her paintings celebrate her country. In her paintings you will find the Mexican flag, temples, clothing, and jewelry. Kahlo also showed her travels and how she felt when she was away from her home. Like Kahlo, make a picture that shows two different places that are important in your life.

1. Choose two places for your picture. Here are some ideas: Did you ever move? Show where you live now and where you used to live. Did your family move to the United States from another country? Is there a special place you like to visit? Perhaps you visit your grandparents in another state or have taken a vacation in an exciting place.

2. Put a photo of yourself in the center of the picture. I used a photograph of me sleeping to show that I am having a dream about my travels.

3. Collect pictures that show each place. Look through travel brochures or use photos you have taken. You can include flags, maps, food, clothing, buildings, or landscapes. I love New York pizza and the Statue of Liberty so I included these for the city. A sun umbrella and an ocean scene tell about my favorite place—the beach.

Supplies

Photograph of you
Magazines and snapshots
Maps
Paper
Scissors
Glue

4. Show a different place on each side. On one side, I showed New York City, where I live in the winter. On the other side, I pasted the beach, where I travel to each summer. I put my dog, Buddy, in both places because I take him with me wherever I go.

Waving flags of my family from Greece and Italy.—Alexi, 8

I live in New York and visit my grandparents in Florida.—Jodi, 9

Flags of Africa and America show my heritage.—Jabari, 9

Me and Myself

In one of her famous paintings, *The Two Fridas*, Kahlo showed herself holding hands with a double of herself! Like Kahlo, make a double self-portrait—a picture that shows two different sides of you. Take two photographs of yourself, or make two drawings. Show yourself with two different feelings. In one, you might be happy; in the other, perhaps you are sad, angry, or frightened. Create a place with magazine collage or paint, and put the two of you in it!

The happy and mad me.—Kirra, 8

Artist Biographies

Salvador Dalí
Spanish, 1904–1989

When Salvador Dalí was a boy, he began drawing and painting. Dalí had confidence in his art and wrote in his diary, "I'll be a great genius." His bold personality sometimes got him into trouble. As a young man, he was expelled from art school for being the ringleader of a student protest.

But Dalí continued making art. In 1929, he joined the Surrealist artists in Paris, who explored the world of dreams and imagination. Dalí painted anything that popped into his head, no matter how silly, weird, or scary it seemed. In his pictures, you will find a woman with drawers coming out of her body, and scary faces that seem to melt. Some people were shocked by Dalí's edgy art and thought it was frightening. Even the leader of the Surrealists, André Breton, eventually rejected Dalí, and Dalí left the group.

He traveled to the United States and became one of the most popular artists of his day. The outrageous stunts he liked to play made him the center of attention, and he often appeared on television. Once he showed up to give an important speech dressed in a diver's suit!

In addition to his art, Dalí also made sculptures, films, photographs, clothing, jewelry, and illustrations, and wrote about his life and ideas. Today he is known as one of the greatest Surrealist artists.

René Magritte
Belgian, 1898–1967

René Magritte was born in a small Belgian town. As a young man, he went to the city of Brussels to study painting. There he lived most of his life with his wife. He painted on an easel in his living room. To earn money, he designed advertising posters. In 1926, he sold his first painting; from then on, he devoted himself to art.

Magritte shared ideas with the Surrealists in Belgium who were interested in making art that puzzles the viewer. In his pictures, he transformed ordinary objects into mysterious scenes by combining things in unusual ways. In one of his famous paintings, a train rushes out of a fireplace. In another, an eyeball peeks out of a plate of food! Magritte also made unusual portraits of himself and his friends. Once he made a picture of himself eating a meal with four arms! Magritte also loved to play with words and confuse their meaning. He painted a pipe and wrote under it, in French, "This is not a pipe."

Later, Magritte lived in Paris, where he met the French Surrealists. He also traveled to London and then returned to Brussels, where he settled. In addition to painting, Magritte made films and took photographs. He was famous during his own lifetime, and today he is known as one of the most important Surrealist artists.

Max Ernst
German, 1891–1976

Max Ernst was born in a small town in Germany. His father painted as a hobby, and Ernst became interested in art as a young boy. He never went to school to learn how to paint. Instead he studied philosophy, psychiatry, and art history at the University of Bonn. There he made friends with many artists and developed his own painting.

During World War I, Ernst served in the German army and was deeply affected by the horrors of war. After the war, he joined a group of artists called the Dadaists. They invented art games and new ways of making art. Ernst created otherworldly magazine collages, and paintings of eerie dreams, creatures, and imaginary places. In 1925, he joined the Surrealist artists in Paris. Like the Surrealists, he wanted to let pictures flow freely from his mind without controlling what they would be. They called this spontaneous way of making art "automatism."

In 1938, Ernst broke away from the Surrealists. Three years later, he moved to New York to escape World War II and later moved to Arizona. There he decorated his house with sculptures and painted landscapes. At the end of his life, he returned to Paris. Ernst became famous in his own lifetime and inspired many younger artists.

Joan Miró
Spanish, 1893–1983

Joan Miró was raised in Catalonian Spain. He and his family often took trips to their farm in Montriog. There Miró enjoyed the peace of country life and the beauty of nature. The plants, animals, insects, stars, moon, and seaside of the country are often shown in his artworks. Miró studied what he saw in nature and painted it as a world filled with imagination. In his paintings, colorful creatures float and faces appear in the night sky. You might see a dog with elephant ears or a fish that seems to fly.

As a young man, Miró went to Paris, France. There he lived and created art most of his life, but occasionally he returned to Spain. In Paris, Miró shared ideas with the Surrealists. They admired Miró's imaginative, free way of making pictures. Miró, however, was not interested in joining the group.

Miró faced difficulties in his life, but no matter what, he continued to make art. At times he was so poor, he barely had enough to eat. Miró was deeply affected by the violence of the Spanish Civil War and World War II. His artworks during these years seem scary and some show monstrous creatures. In addition to painting, he made collages, prints, books, sculptures, and ceramics. During his lifetime, Miró became famous, and today he is known as one of the most important modern artists.

Meret Oppenheim
Swiss, 1913–1983

The Swiss artist Meret Oppenheim was born in Germany. As a young woman, Oppenheim moved to Paris, where she studied art. There she met the Surrealist artists and participated in their exhibitions and meetings. Like the Surrealists, Oppenheim explored the realm of dreams and fantasy.

In 1933, Oppenheim created her first Surrealist sculpture. Rather than make handmade sculptures out of art materials such as clay, metal, or wood, Oppenheim and other Surrealists used actual objects in bizarre ways. Once Oppenheim tied a pair of shoes to a plate and presented it as a sculpture! At age twenty-two, she created her most famous work of art, *Object*. The furry teacup was shown in an important exhibition of Surrealist art at The Museum of Modern Art in New York, and it became one of the most famous Surrealist sculptures.

After her quick rise to fame, the young Oppenheim had difficulty making art and destroyed most of her work from this time. Later in her life, she returned to creating artworks inspired by her earlier ideas. She also worked on special projects such as set designs, costumes, and furniture. Some people disliked her unusual art and were shocked by it. Today, Oppenheim is best known for *Object*—sometimes called *Breakfast with Fur.*

Frida Kahlo
Mexican, 1907–1954

When Frida Kahlo was eighteen years old, she was in a bus accident that left her in pain for the rest of her life. She was forced to remain in bed, recovering, for months. Kahlo's father gave her a box of paints, and her mother brought her a special easel so she could paint from her bed. Kahlo looked in the mirror and painted a picture of herself.

Throughout her life, Kahlo made paintings that tell the story of her memories. She showed her happiest memories, and the sad ones, too. Her pictures celebrate the things that she loved, such as her pet monkeys and her Mexican homeland. In other paintings, she told about her most painful times. For example, she painted herself lying in a hospital bed with tears running down her face. Kahlo married the famous Mexican painter Diego Rivera. The story of their life together, their travels to the United States, and the heartbreak of their divorce are pictured in Kahlo's art.

Kahlo's paintings tell about her memories in an imaginative way. You might see her thoughts floating around her or look right through her body. In 1938, Kahlo had her first exhibition in Europe with the Surrealists. They admired her work for its dreamlike quality. But Kahlo said that her paintings are not about dreams; rather, they tell the true story of her life. Today Kahlo is considered a great painter, and her home in Mexico is now a museum.

About the Author

Joyce Raimondo is director of Imagine That! Art Education, specializing in helping children access the arts. As a visiting author and a consultant to schools, she teaches children how to look at famous artworks and use art history as a springboard for their own creativity. As a consultant, her clients have included *Blues' Clues*, the Children's Television Workshop, and the Pollock-Krasner House and Study Center, among others.

Joyce is author of The Museum of Modern Art's acclaimed Art Safari series of children's books, kits, and online programs. From 1992–2000, she served as family programs coordinator at MoMA in New York, where she created programs that teach children and adults how to enjoy art together.

A painter and sculptor, Joyce's illustrations have been featured in such publications as *The New York Times* and *The Boston Globe*. Her television appearances include *Blue's Clues, Fox Breakfast Time,* and *NBC News,* among others. She divides her time between Manhattan and Amagansett, New York. Visit her on the Web at www.joyceraimondo.com.

Acknowledgments

As director of Imagine That! Art Education, I implement workshops designed to teach children how to enjoy art history. I ask students to describe what they see in famous artworks and follow up with their own creations. Much of the children's art featured in this book was made during these workshops.

A special thanks to the children who contributed artwork: Raquel, Timmy, Raymond, Yanncy, Gabriel, Joshua, Mat, Trevor, Nicole, Thomas Z., Thomas D., Kyle S., Kyle H., Kimberly, Keith, Jana, Austin, Daniela, Christopher D., Antonio, Michael, Emily, Victor, Ben, Rachel, Morrison, Basil, Lauren, Brooke, Lily, Mathew, Christopher S., Madeline, Carrie, Gemma, Britney Mae, Felicia, Erik, Kirra, Chris L., Dawn, Ashley, Sean, Daria, Lucas, Mata, Nhailinger, Laura, Alexi, Jodi, Melissa, Jabari, and Kenneth.

Gratitude is given to my editors, Julie Mazur and Laaren Brown, for bringing clarity to the development of the first volume in the Art Explorers series. I am also thankful to Ed Miller, the designer, who created the book's lively graphics.

Grateful acknowledgment is due to the institutions whose students participated in this project: Amagansett School, Springs School, Victor D'Amico Institute of Art, William S. Covert Elementary, and Woodward Parkway Elementary. I am especially thankful to the administrators and art teachers who welcomed me to their schools: Donna Brittell, Nancy Carney, Elizabeth Clint, Chris Kohan, Darren Raymer, Anita Solovey, Eleanor Tritt, and Ricki Weisfelner. Appreciation is given to the Nassau and Suffolk Boards of Cooperative Education, which funded many of these workshops, and to the coordinators, Jeanette Meoli and Laura Muhs, who arranged them.